Dinosau

Teresa O'Brien

Which dinosaur had three pointed horns on its head?

Like a dragon in a fairy tale this dinosaur had a row of spines down its back. Who could it be?

Which dinosaur had
a long curved crest
on top of its head?

Which dinosaurs can you spot hiding?